O Come, Let Us Adore Him, Christ the Lord

Everybody loves a good story. The more intriguing the plot and characters, the greater our interest. We especially love those dramas that leave us hanging while we must wait to see what happens.

The historical events surrounding the birth of our Lord and Savior Jesus is one such story. *The* story, in fact. Shake from your head that sleepy, almost fairy tale-like Sunday school tale and, instead, picture yourself in the real-life drama of history. Awaken your imagination!

Picture yourself in the room with Mary when Gabriel showed up with a shocking announcement. *Me, Lord?*

Visualize yourself standing in the field at night when the heavens broke open and a million supernatural beings lit up the sky and started shouting. *Glory to God in the highest!*

Imagine being with the old man in the temple when he saw the young couple carrying a baby—and he knew it was the Messiah. *Oh, after so many long years of waiting, he saw Him!*

See yourself sitting with Joseph when he realized he needed to protect his young family from people who wanted to kill the Child. *And they would have had he not done something!*

These are some of the people and events that make this story great—indeed, the greatest story of history. *His* story. At its heart, Christmas is the celebration of *a promise kept.* God's promise to His people that He would provide a Savior. That Savior is His Son, Jesus—God-man, conceived miraculously, taking on human flesh, living among us in order to die in our place. And this is the true account of His miraculous birth—the story that I'd like you to experience in the pages that follow.

I want this book to stir up your imagination by using not only words but also pictures. Some of the photographs are of the actual places where the events occurred. Also included are interesting facts and tidbits about life and culture in Bible times—all intended to stimulate your imagination and your faith.

And so, let us begin! Journey with me through the back window of this familiar scene, and observe it through new eyes. May your faith in the power and grace of our Lord Jesus Christ increase as you revisit the scenes surrounding His birth.

O come, let us adore Him!

Chuck

Charles R. Swindoll

Chuck Swindoll teaching
God's Word in Caesarea, Israel

Jesus's Infant *Journeys*

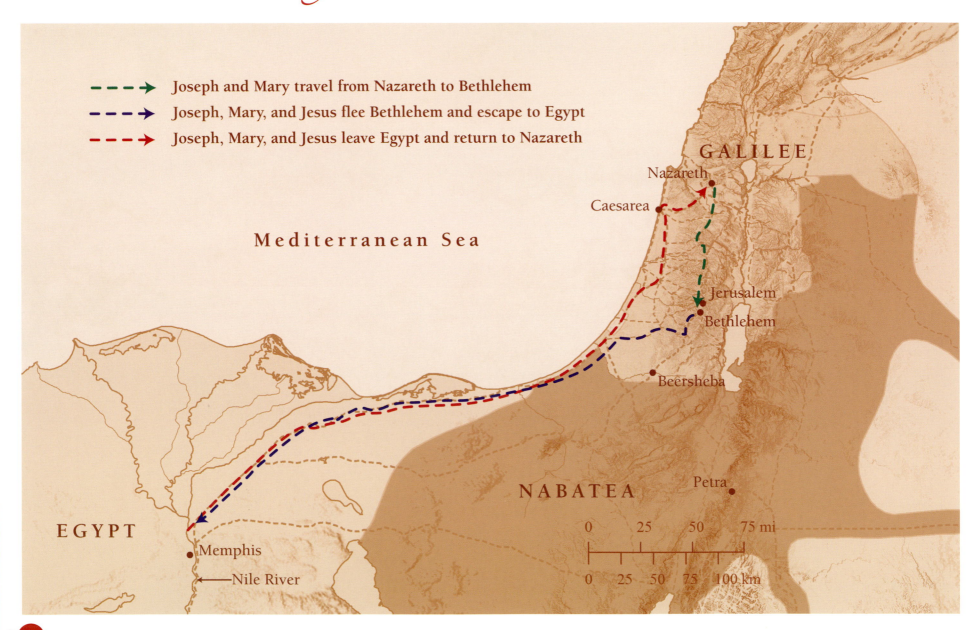

- ━ ➤ Joseph and Mary travel from Nazareth to Bethlehem
- ━ ➤ Joseph, Mary, and Jesus flee Bethlehem and escape to Egypt
- ━ ➤ Joseph, Mary, and Jesus leave Egypt and return to Nazareth

Mediterranean Sea

GALILEE

Nazareth

Caesarea

Jerusalem

Bethlehem

Beersheba

NABATEA

Petra

0   25   50   75 mi

0   25   50   75   100 km

EGYPT

Memphis

Nile River

TABLE OF *Contents*

"*Joy* TO THE WORLD! THE LORD IS *come*; LET EARTH RECEIVE HER *King.*"

As it is written

in the book of the words

of Isaiah the prophet,

"The voice of one crying

in the wilderness,

'Make ready the way
of the LORD,

Make His paths straight.'"

—LUKE 3:4

A typical Roman road which carried the
gospel to the Roman Empire

WATCHING LONG IN HOPE AND FEAR

THE QUESTIONS NAGGED the Jews for the better part of four centuries. Had God forgotten His people? When would He speak again? Would He fulfill His promise and bring salvation to Israel?

After God's prophecy through Malachi, the silence of heaven reigned for four hundred years. Prophets who spoke God's Word to the people of Israel disappeared from the scene. A lack of specific direction or encouragement from God left the Israelites with only one option: they had to trust that God was working in their own era, just as He had in the past.

Indeed, the absence of a prophet indicated God's silence, not His inaction. During the four hundred years after Malachi, God orchestrated political and cultural changes that would prove crucial in ushering in salvation, not just for the Jews but for everyone who placed faith in the babe born in Bethlehem.

The changes began about a century after Malachi prophesied—when a young man named Alexander ascended the throne of the Greek Empire. Alexander extended its borders beyond those of any previous empire, bringing the same Greek language to people as far away as India. After the Greeks fell, the Romans, united under Caesar, built roads and instituted the *Pax Romana*—the peace of Rome—making it easy and safe to travel throughout the empire.

The results of these providential changes? *Pax Romana* kept the magi safe from harm as they traveled along the Roman roads; those same Roman roads got them to Bethlehem in sufficient time to visit the child Jesus. Because a unified language was in place, the New Testament authors were later able to effectively and efficiently tell the whole world the good news about Jesus.

And many faithful Israelites were more ready than ever to receive Him, because for centuries their forefathers had been waiting and hoping in the synagogues, worshiping

The Old Testament was originally written on scrolls.

God their Creator. They would eventually listen as the One would stand and, as Messiah, tell them He had come.

With the coming of Jesus, fear would no longer reign. Hope would be fulfilled. And God would finally break His silence.

See Genesis 49:18; Psalm 62:5; 119:74; Isaiah 64:4; and Luke 4:16–21.

The Hebrews had endured God's silence for a similar period of time during their slavery in Egypt. That silence ended when God raised up a prophet unlike any other before that point in Hebrew history—Moses, who led the people through the Red Sea, delivered them from their captors, proclaimed God's Commandments, and guided them to the Promised Land. God gave Moses the Ten Commandments on Mt. Sinai, in the area pictured above. Later, with the Greeks and then the Romans in power throughout the Promised Land, God's people waited in hope for another, greater prophet—the Messiah (Deuteronomy 18:18–20).

But when *the fullness of the time came,* God sent forth His Son, *born* of a woman, *born* under the Law, so that He might *redeem* those who were under the Law.

—GALATIANS 4:4–5

LATE IN TIME
BEHOLD HIM COME

THE WORD *LUCK* NEVER APPEARS IN SCRIPTURE. Neither does the concept of being "at the right place at the right time"—as if by chance a situation just "works out."

God is at work—behind every scene, shaping every nuance of every event in each of our lives. He's crafting all things to fit together . . . and everything for His purpose.

As tough as that may be to get our minds around, this has always been God's way. Before human history, God had already designed a plan for how we could have a relationship with Him. He knew that, because of our choice to sin, we would be cut off from Him. Holiness cannot tolerate sin. So, at some moment in eternity past, the Lord Jesus, the second member of the Trinity, said yes to the assignment to go to earth. He would become a human, preserved from inherited sin by a virgin conception. He would live a sinless life but pay the highest penalty for sin with His own death. His holy payment would be the only acceptable offering to God for our forgiveness.

As silent as light, God moved from one era to the next, bringing people and events together exactly on schedule. Galatians 4:4 says in "the fullness of the time," which might be paraphrased, "When days and events had run their course and the precise moment was reached, according to God's plan, a Savior emerged on the human scene—Jesus arrived in Mary's womb."

Jesus could have come later—when conditions had been cleaner, when more people could have heard Him firsthand . . . when crucifixion was out of style. But He arrived right on time, in perfect sync with God's purposes.

Skeptics scoff, calling Christians foolish to believe such timing is ordained. But God did time it all. All of time is in God's hands. Take to heart His plan for that thing you wait for today, especially when it feels long overdue. That perfect moment may yet come, when in the fullness of time, God takes action.

See Galatians 4:4.

When was Jesus really born? Theories abound, but according to the best estimate, Jesus most likely was born in the fall or winter of 5 BC. The practice of celebrating Jesus's birth on December 25 began in the AD 300s as a substitute for Saturnalia, an end-of-the-year pagan festival that included decorating one's home with holly, mistletoe, and evergreens and gift-giving, feasting, and drinking. Rather than observing the winter solstice, Christians interchanged celebrating "the unconquerable sun" with celebrating "the Sun of Righteousness," a prophetic nickname for Jesus the Messiah.

Nazareth

Modern-day Nazareth

Modern Nazareth with the Church of the Annunciation at center

NOW IN THE SIXTH MONTH THE ANGEL GABRIEL WAS SENT FROM GOD

TO A CITY IN *Galilee* CALLED *Nazareth*, TO A VIRGIN ENGAGED TO A MAN

WHOSE NAME WAS JOSEPH, OF THE *descendants of David.* —LUKE 1:26–27

PLEASED AS MAN WITH MEN TO DWELL

To say that Mary and Joseph lived in a small country town would be an understatement. Nazareth, then home to no more than three hundred people, would have been more like a first-century "diner and gas truck stop." It sat on a hill just north of the "freeway"—the trade route that moved restless, ceaseless caravans of creaking wagons across the dusty Middle East. A military outpost also camped nearby. Nazareth absorbed the backwash of these transients' immoral habits and profane living. If people had even heard of Nazareth in that day, what they heard wasn't good. No wonder Nathanael curled his lip when he first heard of Jesus: "Can any good thing come out of Nazareth?"

But Nazareth had a little-known secret that fit perfectly in God's plan. According to Bible teacher Ronald Allen, around 100 BC a clan of Jews, newly returned from Babylon, had settled on this hilltop and given it their family name, Natsara. These were the Natsoreans, a Judean family who linked themselves with Isaiah's prophecy, claiming to be in David's line. The townspeople believed that Messiah, the Branch, would be born from their family. To other Jews in larger, more cultured cities, the Natsoreans must have seemed ridiculous in their self-importance.

Quoting Isaiah, Matthew said of Jesus, "He shall be called a Nazarene." More likely he was saying that Jesus would be called a "Natsarene." The difference is just one letter. The New Testament writers used the Greek letter *zeta* in translation of the Hebrew letter that makes a "ts" sound. A Natsarene, "The Branch," echoes Isaiah 11:1:

Then a shoot will spring from the stem of Jesse,
And a branch from his roots will bear fruit.

This great prophecy and promise is answered in Jesus, the Branch from Jesse, from David's line. Jesus would be a "Branch man," from "Branch-town," a secret hidden in the transliteration of one letter.[1]

An obscure town with a bad reputation, Nazareth was God's chosen location to keep a promise. It makes you wonder, when heaven dispatched Gabriel to talk to a teenager about the greatest mission of all time, if Gabriel paused and said, "Really? Nazareth?"

The unfolding of God's mysteries sometimes makes you shake your head and grin.

See Isaiah 11:1; Matthew 2:23; and John 1:46.

Growing up in Nazareth, Jesus learned Joseph's trade. Mark 6:3 says that Joseph was a tekton, translated in many English Bibles as a "carpenter." The word actually means "a craftsman who builds." Considering that Israel's buildings were constructed of stones and rocks, Jesus likely worked as a stonemason. Jesus may have even helped with the construction of nearby Sepphoris (see above), a sophisticated city with modern streets, a theater, and a gymnasium; all were under construction during the time Jesus lived in Nazareth.

The angel answered and said to him, "*I am Gabriel,* who stands in the *presence of God,* and I have been sent to speak to you and to bring you *this good news.*" —Luke 1:19

THE ANGEL GABRIEL FROM HEAVEN CAME

TAKE A TRIP out of time and space.

With the help of your imagination, let yourself be pulled from the gravity of this planet and move into the space beyond the earth's dimension—that mysterious realm where angels dwell.

It's easy to forget we live in two parallel worlds. One is our world . . . tangible and visible—a world of roads and houses and barns and trees and lakes and seas and shores and dogs and cats and days and nights and nations and politicians.

The other unseen world, just as real, is a space we cannot see or touch. It is completely unlike our world. It consists of angels and sinister forces, unseen thrones and ranks of authority. It's a spiritual world where supernatural agents move freely, where battles are fought. Somewhere in that other world are two literal places we have never been: one is heaven and the other is hell. We can't see either and we've never talked to anyone who has been to either place, but they're as real as the world we know—the one we can now touch and feel.

From the spectrum of unapproachable light, God dispatched His angelic courier Gabriel with a communication related specifically to the nation of Israel. Four times that we know of, Gabriel delivered an announcement from God: twice to the prophet Daniel about Israel's future, six earth centuries later to Zacharias about the birth of a little boy named John, and shortly thereafter to Mary to deliver the news of the conception in her womb of the baby Jesus.

Angels are at work today as well, relentlessly busy doing God's bidding in the unseen world around us. If our eyes could be opened to see the angelic forces, we would be overwhelmed! In fact, we'd be thrilled and encouraged to know their number, observe their strength, and realize firsthand their purpose, especially when we are alone and feel a separation from strength ourselves.[2]

See Daniel 8:16; 9:21; Luke 1:19, 26–27; and Hebrews 1:6–14.

Every time Gabriel showed up in the Christmas story, he said, "Do not be afraid"—to Zacharias in the temple and to Mary with the news of her conception. Though not named, perhaps Gabriel was also the angel who comforted Joseph in a dream and the shepherds in the field. Truth be told, when humans are confronted with such otherworldly scenes, "fear not" is easier said than done.

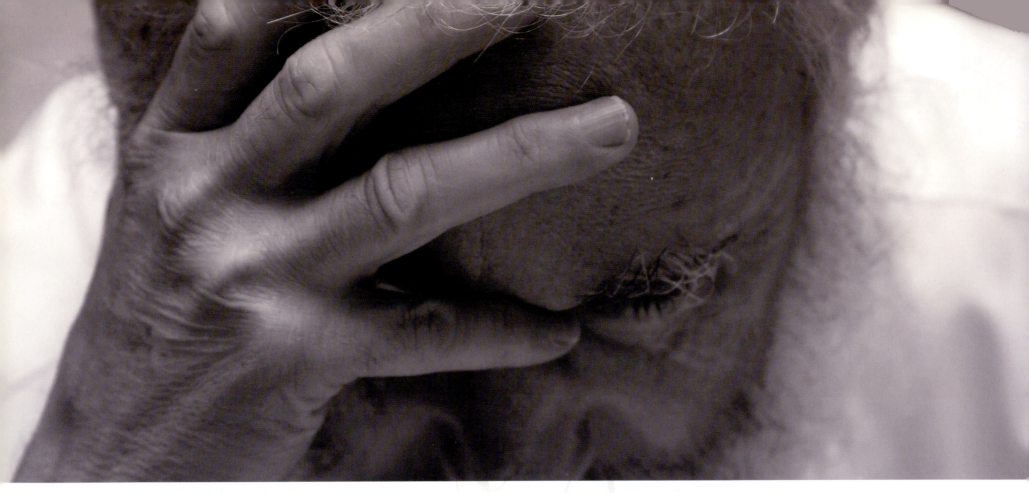

Zacharias, a faithful priest, found faith to be a difficult assignment.

"THE *tender mercy* OF OUR GOD . . . WILL VISIT US,

To *shine* UPON THOSE WHO SIT IN DARKNESS AND THE SHADOW OF DEATH,

To *guide* OUR FEET INTO THE *way of peace.*" —LUKE 1:78–79.

HIS GOSPEL IS PEACE

SILENCE FILLED THE TEMPLE. Zacharias stood mute, the aromatic incense filling his nostrils. His work finished, he staggered out of the Holy Place, the sun shining bright in his eyes. Other priests spoke to him, but just as the angel had said, his tongue was tied.

Despite his verbal predicament, excitement filled Zacharias's heart. Finally, after more than four centuries, God had broken His silence. He had spoken to His people. Only the message had come to Zacharias, who left the temple without the ability to speak himself!

Moments earlier, the angel Gabriel had appeared to the aged priest and prophesied the birth of a son to Zacharias and his then-barren wife, Elizabeth. But Zacharias had doubted the angel. For that, Gabriel had pronounced nine months of silence on the priest. Only when the child, whom they were to name John, was born would God loose Zacharias's tongue.

On the eighth day of the infant John's life, at the ceremony of his circumcision, speech returned to Zacharias once again. The priest, whose name means "God remembers," used his first words to deliver a prophetic word from the Lord, a message that emphasized God's remembrance of His promise to send a deliverer to His people.

Three times in Zacharias's prophecy, the priest recalled the covenants—or promises—that God made to His people: one through Abraham, one through David, and one through Jeremiah. God first promised redemption to Abraham (Luke 1:73; Genesis 15:1–6), later assured His people that salvation would come through a descendant of David (Luke 1:69; 2 Samuel 7:12–16), and eventually pledged that the Deliverer would forgive the sins of God's people (Luke 1:77; Jeremiah 31:31–34).

As Zacharias concluded his prophecy, he affirmed that God would surely visit Israel to shine His light in the darkness and guide His people "into the way of peace." Zacharias knew that at the time of the birth of his son John, the fulfillment of God's promise for a Messiah had already begun. Peace with God for those who believe would soon follow.

Zacharias had been forced into silence for nine months. Now he could be silent no more. The Prince of Peace was indeed coming to the people.

See Luke 1:5–23, 57–80.

When Zacharias entered the temple to perform his priestly service, he was responsible for burning the incense—ketoret in Hebrew. Ketoret is a specific mixture of spices— including stacte, onycha, galbanum, and frankincense—that produces a sweet aroma when burned. The Jews used the mixture only in the temple, setting it apart for the Holy Place where God made His dwelling (Exodus 30:34–38).

Modern Ein Kerem, in the Judean mountains, is likely the site of Zacharias and Elizabeth's home.

"This is the way *the Lord* has dealt with me in the days when He looked with *favor* upon me, to *take away* my *disgrace* among men." —LUKE 1:25

PIERCE THE CLOUDS AND BRING US LIGHT

EMPTY. DISGRACED. BARREN.

The stigma hung over her like a fog. In a culture where children conveyed status, people saw her in a different light, their impressions clouded by her lack of a child rather than illuminated by her commitment to God. In spite of her circumstances, Elizabeth's faith never wavered. She and her husband, Zacharias, were "righteous in the sight of God."

Rather than turn her back on the Lord, this faithful woman dropped to her knees in humility and supplication. She prayed to God for a child. With the storm of personal disappointment and others' criticism bearing down on her, she turned her face toward the only light she could find—the light of God and His grace. Yet despite her pleadings, there the cloud hung, shadowing her every step.

That is, until the day her husband stood in the temple performing his annual priestly service. In that Holy Place, a cloud of incense drifted upward in worship to God. In that moment, the light of God's word delivered to Zacharias by the angel Gabriel pierced the darkness. Elizabeth, now in her old age, would miraculously bear a son. This child, the angel proclaimed, would have the privilege of announcing the coming of the Messiah.

Imagine the tears of joy and relief that poured down Elizabeth's face when she discovered her pregnancy. God had heard her prayers.

Before His lengthy silence—not just to Elizabeth but to all Israel—God had promised His people a Savior, a Messiah. When He broke His four-hundred-year silence through Gabriel's announcement, the Messiah was again the subject of His message. Elizabeth, whose name means "the covenant of my God," stands as a representative of faithful Israel, who had waited so long for their Messiah to come. This small remnant of true believers had, like Elizabeth, prayed to God for deliverance. And like Elizabeth, they had waited. She for a lifetime; they for many generations.

Gabriel's announcement made this truth abundantly clear: God does not forget His promises.

By the announcement of a son who would eventually announce *the* Son, God poured out His mercy onto Israel and onto Elizabeth. No longer surrounded by clouds of disgrace, this faithful woman of God shone bright in the light of rejoicing.

See Luke 1:6, 24–25, 39–45, 57–58.

Elizabeth was not alone. God's grace has worked among infertile women throughout biblical history. Each of the three patriarchs—Abraham, Isaac, and Jacob—was married to a woman who struggled with infertility—Sarai (Genesis 16:1), Rebekah (25:21), and Rachel (29:31). And of course, faithful but childless Hannah came along some time later (1 Samuel 1). In His timing, God blessed each of these women with children.

Mary: trusting God with the impossible

AND MARY SAID, "BEHOLD, THE *bondslave* OF THE LORD;

may it be done TO ME

ACCORDING TO *your word."* —LUKE 1:38

MARY WAS THAT MOTHER MILD

SHE MAY HAVE BEEN IN THE MIDDLE OF MORNING CHORES or perhaps escaping the heat of the day in the family garden. Wherever Mary was, she was probably dreaming of the future—of Joseph . . . their home . . . a family.

Then God interrupted her plans with a plan of His own. *She* would be the one to bear the Messiah, the angel Gabriel told her.

"Do not be afraid, Mary; for you have found favor with God." The thought must have staggered her imagination.

Like every faithful Jewish teenager, she had heard about the promised One who was coming, but to get the news that God had chosen *her* to be the Savior's mother? To have Gabriel announce God's imminent arrival—in her body. . . . *How could this be?* she wondered.

Mary must have realized to some extent that this privilege would come with a high price to her reputation: doubts about her purity, whispers behind veiled glances, icy accusations. *Who did she say was the father?*

But Mary responded immediately in faith to what she could not understand.

Without any delay, she responded in submission to whatever God wanted. "May it be to me as you have said," Mary said. The Greek word *ginomai* used in this verse, which means "turn out to be," is a word of surrender, in the sense of let it "happen" or let it be.[3] We could translate Mary's response as, "I don't fully understand this, but I accept it. I know it will happen just as Gabriel said."

It was enough for her that God had promised to perform the impossible.

It was enough for her that God had entrusted to her this privilege.

She would trust Him with the rest.

The angel had said that the One who would be conceived in her was greater than anything she had ever dreamed—greater than anything this earth had ever known. The plot set in motion that day, planned before time began, was a promise kept—the promise of relief, of salvation to all who would believe.

See Luke 1:30, 38 (NIV) and Luke 1:46–55.

Expectant mothers hold a special place in God's program. Perhaps they uniquely realize that the mystery forming in their bodies is their only opportunity to partner with God in the miracle of life. When Mary heard of her miraculous conception, she ran to her cousin, whom Mary had heard was also pregnant. They praised God together for His special purposes being formed in their wombs. Mary sang a beautiful poem recalling more than twelve Old Testament references. Her obvious love for God and His Word intricately wove itself in her thoughts in this tender time.

Joseph: a man of honor, faith, and courage

An angel of the Lord appeared to him in a dream. . . .

And *Joseph* awoke from his sleep and *did as the angel of the Lord commanded him*, and took Mary as his wife, but kept her a virgin until she gave birth to a Son; and he called His name Jesus. —Matthew 1:20, 24–25

JOSEPH DEAREST, JOSEPH MINE

To JOSEPH, MARY'S SURPRISE PREGNANCY must have felt like a train wreck. The woman he loved—the one to whom he had pledged his commitment before God and man, the one he had kept pure despite his own desires—disappeared for three months and then showed up again pregnant. *What was he supposed to think?*

He didn't believe her. It tore him apart, but he just couldn't wrap his mind around Mary's story. He needed a plan. By law he could break their betrothal commitment. By the letter of the law, he could have her stoned to death as an adulterer. But he loved her, so he would preserve whatever dignity she had left and "send her away secretly." Terminating Mary's pregnancy never crossed anyone's mind. Mary would just go away . . . and raise the child alone.

At least that's what Joseph had decided as he went to bed one restless night. But God intervened, dispatching an angel, Gabriel most likely, to visit Joseph in a dream and say, "Do not be afraid to take Mary as your wife; for the Child who has been conceived in her is of the Holy Spirit."

Joseph believed God. His faith put his frantic plans to rest. He would agree to be Mary's support and strength in this wonderful and wounding experience.

From that day forward, we meet a faithful, humble man, protecting Mary and this child that was not his own. Providing for them. Obeying God. In the simple act of naming the child *Jesus* (and not after himself, which was the tradition for firstborn sons), Joseph told the world that this child was not his. In that one dream, he caught a vision for his role in this magnificent mission, and it both energized and humbled him. When he realized the challenge of it, he stepped up.

In every way, Joseph played the role of surrogate dad—teaching Jesus His trade, training Him in the

Craftsmen tools as would have been used in a first-century shop

Law and the Prophets as did every good Jewish father. How was Joseph's life impacted by the hours with his "Son"? We cannot know.

We know only this—that the power of Joseph's choice to believe that God's promise was being fulfilled changed the course of his life. We face such decisions of faith in large and small ways today—decisions that, once made, change the direction of our lives.

See Matthew 1:18–25 and Leviticus 20:10.

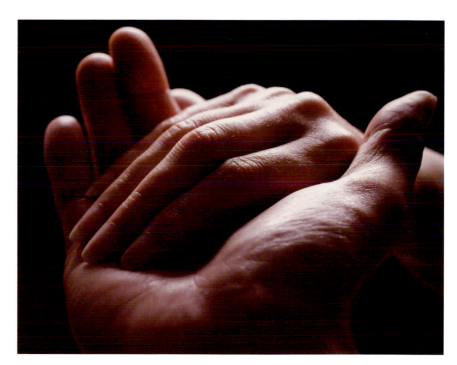

Wedding customs in first century BC began with a "betrothal" period. This was something like an engagement, but a betrothal carried the finality of marriage. The young couple, usually between ages 13 and 15, registered publicly in the synagogue as man and wife, though the ceremony was still twelve months away. This betrothal time was spent building a small home and shopping for furniture. The only way to break a betrothal was by divorce or death.

For a child will be born to us,
a son will be given to us;
And the government will rest on His shoulders;
And His name will be called

Wonderful

COUNSELOR

mighty

God

Eternal Father

Prince of Peace

— Isaiah 9:6

Jesus, Our Emmanuel

At Christmas, we celebrate Jesus's entrance on the human scene. However, Jesus has been active since before His birth, weaving His promises and their fulfillment through every chapter of humanity's existence. The Bible is proof of this—picturing Jesus in every book.

In **Genesis**, Jesus is the promise of blessing upon humanity.

In **Exodus**, Jesus is the Passover Lamb, the promise of redemption.

In **Leviticus**, Jesus is the promised sacrifice in fulfillment of God's laws.

In **Numbers**, Jesus is the promise of healing, pictured in the serpent lifted up in the desert.

In **Deuteronomy**, Jesus is the promised Prophet yet to come.

In **Joshua**, Jesus brings promised "salvation"—the meaning of His name.

In **Judges**, Jesus is the ultimate Judge.

In **Ruth**, Jesus fulfills the promise of the kinsman-redeemer.

In **1** and **2 Samuel**, **1** and **2 Kings**, and **1** and **2 Chronicles**, Jesus is pictured as the promised King.

In **Ezra** and **Nehemiah**, Jesus brings His people back to the Promised Land.

In **Esther**, Jesus is the Advocate, willing to die for His people.

In **Job**, Jesus is our Mediator, Redeemer, and Intercessor.

In **Psalms**, Jesus is our King and Shepherd.

In **Proverbs**, Jesus is the promise of wisdom which is the pattern to a godly life.

In **Ecclesiastes**, Jesus is the one Shepherd who offers abundant life.

In the **Song of Solomon**, Jesus is the Lord who blesses marital intimacy.

In the **Prophets**, Jesus is the promised Prince of Peace and Suffering Servant.

In **Matthew**, Jesus is the promised King of the Jews.

In **Mark**, Jesus fulfills the promise of the Suffering Servant.

In **Luke**, Jesus is God's ideal Man.

In **John**, Jesus is the Son of God.

In **Acts**, Jesus sends His promised Spirit.

In **Romans**, Jesus is the promise of salvation.

In **1 Corinthians**, Jesus promises spiritual gifts to His followers, the church.

In **2 Corinthians**, Jesus provides promised strength in weakness.

In **Galatians**, Jesus is the promised source of power to live by grace.

In **Ephesians**, Jesus is the model of spiritual maturity.

In **Philippians**, Jesus is the fountain of promised joy.

In **Colossians**, Jesus has first place in everything.

In **1** and **2 Thessalonians**, Jesus promises to come back for His people.

In **1** and **2 Timothy**, Jesus promises to be our Mediator.

In **Titus**, Jesus promises to redeem and purify His people.

In **Philemon**, Jesus is the One in whom we have the promise of reconciliation and forgiveness.

In **Hebrews**, Jesus is the promised author and finisher of our faith.

In **James**, Jesus is the inspiration behind our deeds of faith.

In **1** and **2 Peter**, Jesus promises to be our Shepherd and rescuer.

In **1**, **2**, and **3 John**, Jesus promises His saving life.

In **Jude**, Jesus is the promised Judge of false prophets.

In **Revelation**, Jesus is our promise fulfilled, King of Kings and Lord of Lords.

The record of the genealogy of *Jesus the Messiah,* the *son of David,* the *son of Abraham.* —MATTHEW 1:1

O Come, Thou Key of David, Come

Everyone has roots. People since Adam and Eve have studied their family trees to learn from and establish identity with those who have gone before.

When it comes to Jesus, we can easily forget or even discount His human roots and identity—at least when we get beyond His mother, Mary. As a fully human being, Jesus had deep ancestral roots, a family history that the Bible records in Matthew 1 and Luke 3.

These gospel genealogies take us through Old Testament history, naming men and women, well-known and obscure, who hold a place in the lineage of the Messiah.

Key figures such as Abraham and David appear in both passages, connecting Jesus to two of the most significant people—and covenants—in Jewish history. As a descendant of Abraham, Jesus became the fulfillment of Abraham's covenant, the One through whom God would bless the whole world (Genesis 12:2–3).

And Jesus's connection to David takes on great biblical significance, both in the Old Testament and in the New. In His covenant with David, God promised the son of Jesse that a descendant would reign on his throne forever (2 Samuel 7:16). After that promise, the people of Israel waited for a Messiah from the line of David, a ruler who would finally crush their enemies and bring lasting deliverance. Isaiah expressed this longing by referring to a future ruler of Israel as "the key of the house of David" (Isaiah 22:22), a phrase that Jesus later used in reference to Himself (Revelation 3:7).

The genealogies retain their significance not simply because they remind us of the longing and waiting of the Old Testament Israelites. They assure us that the One who has long since made His sacrifice is and was the promised Messiah, the fulfillment of prophecy, the King of Kings. They make clear that God is as good as His word. When He makes a promise, He keeps it.

Generations pass, some good and others evil. Times of darkness may encroach on our lives and threaten to dim our hope. But as you read the genealogies of Jesus, remember God's unending faithfulness to bring about His purposes in His time.

See Matthew 1:1–17 and Luke 3:23–38.

Have you ever noticed the differences in Jesus's genealogies from Matthew and Luke? Why, for instance, is the son of David different in each genealogy (compare Matthew 1:6 and Luke 3:31)? Most scholars explain the difference by suggesting that Matthew recorded Joseph's genealogy, while Luke recorded Mary's. Scholars base this view on Luke's emphasis on Mary's story, as well as his qualifying remark "as was supposed" in reference to Joseph as the father of Jesus (Luke 3:23).

AND WE KNOW THAT

God CAUSES ALL THINGS

to work together FOR GOOD

TO THOSE WHO LOVE GOD,

TO THOSE WHO ARE CALLED

according to

His purpose.

—ROMANS 8:28

Commemorative statue of Caesar Augustus, sculpted by Hubert Gerhard. This statue stands in Augsburg, the second oldest city in Germany. Augsburg is named after Caesar Augustus, the first emperor of the Roman Empire.

SOVEREIGN FATHER, HEAVENLY KING

THAT FIRST CHRISTMAS, ALL EYES WERE ON AUGUSTUS —the cynical Caesar who demanded a census so as to determine a measurement to enlarge taxes even further. At such a time, who was interested in a young couple making an eighty-mile trip south from Nazareth? What could possibly be more important than Caesar's decisions in Rome . . . or his puppet Herod's edicts in Judea? Who cared about a tiny baby born to an unknown teenage Jewess in an obscure Bethlehem barn?

God did.

Without realizing it, mighty Augustus was only an errand boy for the commencement of the fullness of time. He was a pawn in the hand of God . . . a mere piece of lint on the pages of prophecy. While Rome was busy making history, God arrived. The world didn't even notice. Reeling from the wake of Alexander the Great . . . Herod the Great . . . and Augustus the Great, the world overlooked Jesus the baby.

It still does.

As in Jesus's day, our times are desperate. Moreover, they are often a *distraction* from the bigger picture. Just as the political, economical, and spiritual crises of the first century set the stage for "the fullness of time" to occur . . . so today, in our own desperate times, our God is weaving His sovereign tapestry to accomplish His divine will. Times are hard, indeed — but they never surprise God. He is *still* sovereign. He is *still* enthroned.

Christmas is an excellent time to ask ourselves this question: *Will I focus on Jesus as the center of my life and cling to Him, regardless of the circumstances I face?*

Ancient Roman denarius coins

Political corruption . . . religious compromise . . . economic crises — these will always be on the front page. But we must remember that our God is at work on every page. His picture never appears, but His fingerprints are all over the map.

He promises to use our uncertain times to accomplish His bigger and better purposes all around our world . . . and deep within our lives.[4]

See Romans 8:28–30.

This mausoleum in Rome is Caesar Augustus's burial place. First-century Rome commanded a census, the purpose of which was to provide a list for levying taxes. Both Mary and Joseph descended from King David, and so both journeyed to the city from which David's family came — Bethlehem. From humankind's perspective, the census was merely a greedy, political move . . . Caesar wanted money. But God was using humanity's plans for His own purposes — which He had intended long ago (Micah 5:2).

Bethlehem

A panoramic view of Bethlehem

Olive groves outside of Bethlehem

"But as for you, *Bethlehem* Ephrathah, Too little to be among the clans of Judah,

From you *One will go forth for Me* to be ruler in Israel.

His goings forth are from long ago, From the days of eternity." —Micah 5:2

O LITTLE TOWN OF BETHLEHEM

WHEN WE LISTEN TO CHRISTMAS CAROLS and look at Christmas cards, we often find them filled with sentimental terms such as *tidings*, *goodwill*, *noel*, *cheer*, and *Merry Christmas*. Scenes on the cards typically depict a newborn with radiant beams on His holy face, oxen and donkeys bowing, and halos hovering above Jesus, Joseph, and Mary. We refer to the baby's bed as a "manger," not a feed trough. We call the scene a "nativity," not a birth. We've even built a church over the cave where Christ was born! We do all we can *to take away* the ignobility the Bible explicitly portrays. Namely, Jesus Christ's birth represented humility in the truest sense of the word.

Seven hundred years before the birth of Christ, Micah prophesied that One coming from eternity would bring the Hebrews back to their land and rule Israel with worldwide fame in the strength of the Lord. This mighty Messiah would come from the ignoble, little town of Bethlehem.

Why such unadorned humility? From His cradle to His cross, Jesus embraced the indignity we deserved . . . so that we might live with Him in glory.

Jesus came the first time to live the perfect life each of us should have lived . . . and to die the death each of us should have died for our sins. The *second* coming of Christ is the one everyone wanted first—the coming in which the Messiah rules as King over all. While Micah blended both advents into one prophecy, we understand the necessity of their separation (Hebrews 9:28). The only way we could ever have peace on earth and goodwill among us was for the sin among us to be removed.

We needed a Savior before we needed a King.

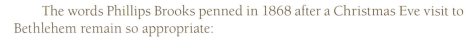

The words Phillips Brooks penned in 1868 after a Christmas Eve visit to Bethlehem remain so appropriate:

> In thy dark streets shineth
> The everlasting Light:
> The hopes and fears of all the years
> Are met in thee tonight.[1]

See Micah 5:2–5.

Wheat fields in Israel have fed God's people for generations. Bethlehem's name means "House of Bread."

The first part of Scripture mentions Bethlehem in conjunction with idolatry, rape, and murder. Not a great beginning for the little town of Bethlehem! But like a shaft of light in the darkness, the city became the hometown of a godly foreigner named Ruth, who became the great-grandmother of King David. Bethlehem became known as the "City of David," and the Messiah, the son of David, would be born there (Micah 5:2).

*"[Mary] wrapped Him in cloths,
and laid Him in a manger"
(Luke 2:7).*

The angel answered and said to her, "The *Holy Spirit* will *come upon you,* and the power of the Most High will overshadow you; and for that reason the *holy Child* shall be called the *Son of God.*" —LUKE 1:35

OFFSPRING OF THE VIRGIN'S WOMB

"A VIRGIN WILL BE WITH CHILD."

Words seem quaint in the face of a promise and a mystery as great as the virgin birth. So many events in biblical history have parallels either in the biblical record or in everyday life. But the virgin birth is one of the few that remains completely singular.

And rightly so.

The Bible says that the Holy Spirit came upon Mary and that she became pregnant as a result. Rather than take this in a sexual manner, these words simply affirm the Holy Spirit's active, creative power. Just as God breathed life into Adam at creation and into Jesus at the resurrection; so, too, the Lord breathed life into Mary's womb. No doubt Mary was humbled in the face of such a miracle, but no more so than when faced with the reality of the fruit of her womb: Jesus, God come to earth in human flesh.

The birth united Jesus with the rest of humanity, making Him a descendant of the first human, Adam. God created Adam from the dust of the newly formed ground—untilled, virgin soil. Just as Adam was formed directly by God, so was the body of Jesus in Mary's womb.

Jesus, then, became a second Adam. Instead of falling into sin and bringing condemnation on humanity as Adam did, Jesus lived a perfect existence and brought redemption to the world (Romans 5:19). Where the first Adam failed to keep humanity's relationship with God secure, Jesus, the second Adam, renewed that relationship.

However, Jesus was not just another human. Jesus's mother being a *virgin* set Him apart from all humanity and indicated His divine nature. Jesus was a man, yes, but different from all people because He was also God.

The virgin birth remains one of the greatest mysteries in all of human history. And while mystery can be a difficult reality for us to accept, it can also direct our eyes heavenward to Him whose thoughts are beyond our own (Isaiah 55:8). When God caused Isaiah to prophesy that a virgin would bear a child and call His name Immanuel, the Lord already knew how He planned to deliver humanity, even if no one else did. And, once again, He fulfilled His promise.

See Isaiah 7:14 and Matthew 1:18–25.

One early and popular extrabiblical Christian tradition holds that Mary's parents were named Joachim and Anna. The couple married young but, like the biblical figures Zacharias and Elizabeth, spent many years childless. Only after they had offered countless prayers were they rewarded with their daughter Mary. Like Hannah did with Samuel, Joachim and Anna dedicated Mary to the service of God.

"Joseph also went up from Galilee . . . to the city of David which is called Bethlehem" (Luke 2:4).

WHILE THEY WERE [IN BETHLEHEM], THE DAYS WERE COMPLETED FOR HER TO GIVE BIRTH.

AND *she gave birth to her firstborn son*; AND SHE WRAPPED HIM IN CLOTHS,

AND LAID HIM IN A MANGER, BECAUSE THERE WAS NO ROOM FOR THEM IN THE INN.   —LUKE 2:6–7

THE WONDER OF IT ALL

WHEN MARY AND JOSEPH BEGAN THEIR JOURNEY southward to Bethlehem, they probably thought they had time to make the trip, register for the census, and then return home to Nazareth before the baby would be born. The weather cooperated and a donkey carried their provisions, but the journey proved more lengthy than either of them had expected. Mary was soon to give birth.

By the time they reached Bethlehem, Mary was exhausted. To make matters worse, the tiny town was packed with travel-weary people. Joseph searched for lodging . . . nothing. One kind family agreed to let them stay in a stable. It was a crude shelter, but it kept them out of the elements. No doubt a low fire warmed the chilly night air.

Once they were settled, Mary rested while Joseph worked his way through the corrupt registration process. Too soon, a powerful, dull ache gripped Mary's abdomen. She called out for Joseph in a panic, but he would be gone for hours. She had attended many childbirths, so she calmed herself and arranged their little shelter in preparation for the baby. A spare tunic would be His swaddling; a little bed of fresh straw in the feeding trough would cradle the newborn infant.

As evening fell, her labor pains intensified and accelerated. Joseph returned from the city tax office to find Mary moaning through a bone-deep wave of pain. There are no pains like those of childbirth. None so intense. None so hopeful.

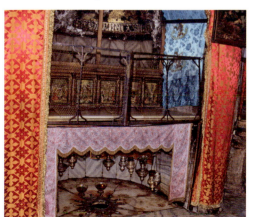

Perhaps it was well into the night when Joseph laid the tiny Hope of Israel in Mary's arms. For nine months prior to His birth, Mary had talked to the baby, sung to Him, felt His body move, and looked forward to the day when she could finally touch Him. Now she looked into His eyes—Immanuel, "God with us."

In Bethlehem's modern Church of the Nativity, a star on the floor marks the traditional location of the birth of Jesus.

It's hard to know if, in those first hours, God gave Mary a brief premonition of years to come, when another would point to her Son and say, "Behold, the Lamb of God who takes away the sin of the world!" . . . or when that promise would be fulfilled and a sword of emotion would pierce her own soul. Anticipated or not, those days would surely come. Mary's little Lamb was destined for sacrifice. But tonight she held her baby close, kissed his soft cheek . . . and wept quietly in the wonder of it all.[2]

See Matthew 1:23; John 1:29; and Luke 2:35.

Think of the first time they heard the voice of God through a human throat, the first time they saw God's tears, the first time they, alone together, studied the face of this miracle baby. Joseph looked and saw none of his resemblance. Mary looked and saw God. Pause and take in the wonder of this scene. This young couple, though they were most likely dazed and overwhelmed, were the first to witness the magnificent truth of John 1:14, "And the Word became flesh, and dwelt among us, and we saw His glory."

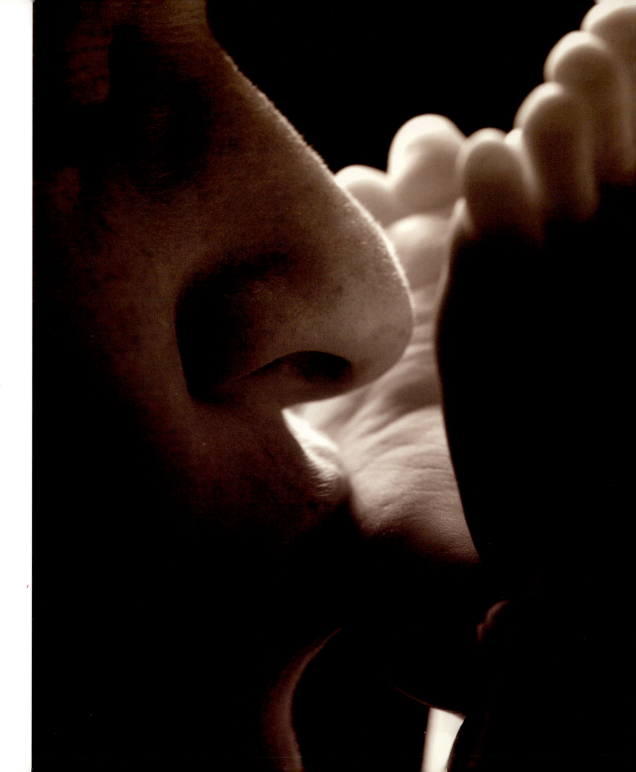

MARY *treasured*

ALL THESE THINGS,

pondering them

IN HER HEART.

—LUKE 2:19

Mary, Did You Know?

Twenty Questions for Mary

What did it feel like to hear that you were the one chosen by God to be the Messiah's mom? Did you ever wonder, *why me*?

• Were you surprised the first time you felt the flutter of life in your body?

• How did your parents react when you told them about Gabriel's visit and announcement?

• Did you cry when Elizabeth greeted you so warmly?— *She knew!* Did you compare food cravings, morning sickness, swollen ankles?

• Was telling Joseph your news the hardest thing you've ever done? Were you fearful that you would have to raise this baby alone?

How did you deal with the spiteful looks and words of criticism from the women in Nazareth?

• Did you *have* to go with Joseph to Bethlehem, or did you just not want to be without him in Nazareth?

• Did you count newborn Jesus's fingers and toes? Whom did He look like? Did He have your nose or your eyes?

• Did you mind the clumsy intrusion of the shepherds into your makeshift birthing room? What did you think of their story about the angels in the field?

• How did Joseph act with baby Jesus? Did he mind naming him Jesus, rather than Joe Jr.? Did he pick Jesus up when He cried? Did you ever eavesdrop on him talking privately to baby Jesus? What did he say?

When did Jesus first sleep through the night? What songs did you sing to Him during 3 a.m. feedings?

• What about Simeon in the temple? Did you wonder how the old priest knew your boy was the Messiah? And what did you think about his odd prediction about the sword?

What was it like to know that someone wanted to kill your baby? Did you weep and pray for the mothers whose babies were murdered in the search for yours?

• Did your heart ache to leave God's Land and move to Egypt? Were you proud of the way Joseph protected you and Jesus?

• What was it like to raise a kid who didn't sin? Did you feel guilty every time you did?

What were Jesus's first words? His favorite foods? Did He have a pet?

• Did you ever keep Jesus's fingers away from Joseph's spikes and hammers only to stop and ponder the future?

• As you watched Jesus mature, did you see Him growing in the realization of His Father's business?

Did you ever cry to God for help in knowing how to be Jesus's mom? Did you ever feel like God should have chosen someone else? Someone older? Someone wiser? Someone who could have given Jesus a better life?

Did you ever look at this sweet little boy, God's little boy, and ponder the amazing truth that He was the Christ, the Messiah, the Savior of the world . . . and that He was *your* Savior?

Bethlehem flocks provided the lambs for sacrifices performed in the nearby Jerusalem temple.

"TODAY *in the city of David* THERE HAS BEEN BORN FOR YOU A SAVIOR,

WHO IS CHRIST THE LORD. . . .

YOU WILL FIND A BABY WRAPPED IN CLOTHS AND LYING *in a manger.*" —LUKE 2:11–12

TO CERTAIN POOR SHEPHERDS

THE MERCHANT SHOPS OF MODERN BETHLEHEM make use of the town's most famous event in history by selling various olive wood nativity sets and Christmas paraphernalia. But just east of the city lies a large pasture known as "The Shepherds' Field." Here, the modern traveler can exchange Christmas shopping for the Christmas story. No olive wood sets . . . just olive trees. No merchants hawking trinkets . . . just local children holding lambs in their arms. This rocky meadow represents the likely location of the angel's announcement to the shepherds on that first Christmas night.

The shepherds guarded flocks of sheep that were raised for sacrifice in Jerusalem. The words they heard from the angelic herald—"Today in the city of David there has been born for you a Savior, who is Christ the Lord"—gave a glimpse of what salvation would cost: *the babe in the manger would become the final sacrificial Lamb.* Jesus—just like the flocks the shepherds pastured that night—was born to die in Jerusalem, only five miles up the road from Bethlehem.

As the herdsmen hurried into Bethlehem to find the baby, the wonder of God's power must have seemed a strange contradiction to the conditions they found. Two thousand years of waiting for the Messiah, and He was born in a barn and laid in a feed trough! *We* would have given God's Son a room in the finest, five-star hotel in Bethlehem. But Jesus got only a one-star motel—and God had to provide the star!

Scripture reveals that "God has chosen the foolish things of the world to shame the wise," and Jesus Himself prayed as an adult, "I praise you, Father, Lord of heaven and earth, because you have hidden these things from the wise and learned, and revealed them to little children."

Why would the Lord first announce the Messiah's birth to lowly shepherds? Why would God choose such an ignoble beginning for such an important birth? Perhaps for the same reason He would choose such an ignoble death for such an exemplary life: *we—lowly sinners—needed a Savior.*

All who heard the shepherds' story listened in wonder at their words.

And we're still marveling.[3]

See Luke 2:11, 18; 10:21 (NIV); and 1 Corinthians 1:27.

A modern shepherd keeps his flock behind a rock wall near Bethlehem. The wall offers shelter and security for the flock. By sleeping in the gap of the wall, the shepherd serves as the "gate"—a custom also common in Jesus's day. In fact, the Lord used this custom to illustrate the security of salvation He would provide: "I am the gate; whoever enters through me will be saved. . . . My sheep listen to my voice. . . . I give them eternal life, and they shall never perish; no one can snatch them out of my hand" (John 10:9, 27–28 NIV).

"*Behold*, THE *virgin* SHALL BE WITH CHILD AND SHALL *bear a Son*,

AND THEY SHALL CALL HIS NAME *Immanuel*,"

WHICH TRANSLATED MEANS, "*God with us*." —MATTHEW 1:23

HAIL THE INCARNATE DEITY

ON THAT STILL WINTER'S NIGHT, SOMETHING WAS UP . . . something extraordinary . . . something supernatural. The shepherds raced to the City of David and found their Savior, just as the angel had said . . . swaddled and lying in a feeding trough. This was the Promised One, the Messiah! God had finally come to dwell with His people, but in such an unexpected way.

Just who was this holy Child the shepherds gazed upon? Make no mistake: He was incarnate deity. The newborn Jesus existed in eternity past as God the Son. He was coequal, coeternal, and coexistent with God the Father and God the Holy Spirit. However, Jesus relinquished the privileges and the pleasures of His existence in heaven when He took upon Himself the limitations of humanity (Philippians 2:6–7). In emptying Himself, Jesus voluntarily set aside the prerogatives and prerequisites of life as He had known it, an existence He had enjoyed; He released His right to that kind of life, saying to the Father, "I will go."

Go where? To Bethlehem. He took "the form of a bond-servant, and [was] made in the likeness of men." Allow yourself to picture what the shepherds saw. There He is, the baby. Do you see His ten fingers and ten toes? His button nose? Can you hear the cries? There's humanity. In this holy infant is the beginning of an earthly life. Look deep into His eyes and see the beginning of life itself.

Later, this divine man, completely unique in His nature and in the perfect life that He lived, "humbled Himself by becoming obedient to the point of death, even death on a cross." Isn't that amazing? Of all ways to die, He died on a cross—the most humiliating and painful kind of death.

God the Son lowered Himself. He took on the flesh of an infant. He died a humiliating death. As a result, God the Father "highly exalted Him." One day, all will bow in worship of the risen Lord, "to the glory of God the Father."

It's all about His glory. What a plan. What an execution. What a perfect, awesome wrapping! The God-man. Jesus is undiminished deity and true humanity, two distinct natures in one person, forever. That's the baby in the manger![4]

See Isaiah 7:14 and Philippians 2:5–11.

Seven hundred years before Jesus's birth, Isaiah prophesied that one called Immanuel— God with us—would be born (Isaiah 7:14). Jesus, the subject of that promise, was the child born to save humanity from its sins (Matthew 1:21). With such a mission before Him, Jesus had to be divine. His deity gave Him the ability to save us. His humanity gave Him the ability to die, after having lived a perfect life. Only Jesus, the God-man, could offer this eternal salvation.

AND THERE WAS A MAN

IN JERUSALEM WHOSE

NAME WAS *Simeon*;

AND THIS MAN WAS RIGHTEOUS

AND DEVOUT,

LOOKING FOR THE

consolation of Israel;

AND THE HOLY SPIRIT WAS

UPON HIM.

—LUKE 2:25

God gave Simeon a very special promise.

THE HOPES AND FEARS OF ALL THE YEARS

TIME WAS RUNNING OUT FOR SIMEON. God had told the devout Jew that he wouldn't die until he'd seen the Messiah with his own two eyes. Day after day Simeon showed up in the temple, petitioning God for Israel's sake, studying each young boy, every baby—*Are you the Messiah?* Simeon was sure he would know the Messiah when he saw Him. His expectation had only increased as the years had flown by. *God had better hurry*, he must have said with a chuckle in lighter moments.

Imagine the moment, then, when Simeon looked up from his temple post and saw the young couple crossing the courtyard. One cradled the baby; the other carried the basket with two pigeons for sacrifice. The Spirit of God whispered, *There He is!* and Simeon's heart soared. *Messiah!*

The couple no doubt felt strange having their secret out; they knew their boy was special . . . from God . . . but now a perfect stranger wept as he held out his arms. *May I hold Him?*

Simeon cried in praise:

"Now Lord, You are releasing Your bond-servant to depart
   in peace,
According to Your word;
For my eyes have seen Your salvation."

Six weeks in the world, the wide-eyed baby thrashed His limbs in excitement. Perhaps Mary's and Joseph's eyes met, still shy to all this attention.

Then something about Mary stopped Simeon; his expression changed. Something more was happening in this interaction than a promise kept between God and an old man. As Simeon handed Jesus back to Mary, a shadow moved across his face. What Simeon saw was a long way off, but it was as real as the relief he felt that day.

"Behold, this Child is appointed for the fall and rise of many in Israel . . . and a sword will pierce even your own soul."

Grief . . . it seems so out of place in this joyful season. Yet Simeon couldn't escape the intimate connection between the Messiah's arrival and the suffering to come: a mother's heart pierced . . . a nation's divided choice . . . a sacrifice beyond words. One has to wonder what Simeon saw coming.

Jesus met the hopes and fears of all the years for which Simeon—and all the faithful of Israel—had waited. Redemption had come to Israel . . . but at an immense cost.

See Luke 2:26, 29–30, 34–35.

A month after Jesus was born, Joseph and Mary observed two important ceremonies in Jewish Law. Redemption of the firstborn: every firstborn male belonged to God, in remembrance of God saving their sons in Egypt on Passover. Parents symbolically bought back their sons from God for five shekels each. Purification after childbirth: a woman was considered unclean for forty days after childbirth. She then brought to the temple a lamb for a burnt offering. If she couldn't afford a lamb, she could bring two pigeons. That is what Mary did—a clear sign that Jesus was born into a very ordinary home.

His *mother treasured* ALL THESE THINGS *in her heart.* —LUKE 2:51

LIKE MARY, LET US PONDER

MARY HAD A FRONT-ROW SEAT to the whole Christmas story. The gospel writer Luke relied on Mary's memories to craft the intimate details of his gospel. Twice in chapter 2 we read that Mary "treasured all these things"—once as she recalled the events surrounding Jesus's birth and then twelve years later when she experienced Jesus breaking boyhood ties with her and Joseph. Who other than Mary could have supplied those details? If she had kept a baby book, Mary's reflections would have filled the pages with milestones and mysteries of Jesus's young life—sweet things He said and did, private and personal moments that stole her mother-heart. As far as we know, Mary kept these treasured memories to herself. How like many of our own mothers, who loved us in ways we cannot know.

Of all people, Mary knew Jesus's significance. But perhaps not fully. Did she know He would be executed on a cross? No—though she no doubt played out in her mind Simeon's prophecy over and again, pondering what he might have meant by "a sword will pierce even your own soul." Did she know Jesus was the Savior of the world? Perhaps, though Jewish tradition held that the Savior wielded a political sword, not a spiritual one.

Mary saw through a glass darkly. But one thing is clear—Mary couldn't keep her eyes off of Jesus from the moment she first saw Him in the shadows of a dim lantern light to even the hour He hung on a cross a lifetime later. She was one favored by God to play an ordinary mom's role to a supernatural Son in an extraordinary season.

Perhaps as Mary sat with Luke years later, years after she had watched Jesus ascend into heaven, time stood still in her memory. No doubt she still pondered the events of her life, then with the wisdom of hindsight. Then, every moment she had spent with Jesus was even more treasured. And perhaps, if she sat especially quiet, she could still hear His voice echoing across the years:

Mommy, help me lace my sandals. Mom, what's for dinner? Woman, don't you know my time is not yet come? Mom, behold your son. . . . Mom, I'll be back.

See Luke 2:19, 35, 51.

The Christmas story is, of all things, a human story. Jesus took on human form. Humans reacted. A doubting Zacharias, a devastated Joseph choosing to divorce the one he loved, a trusting Mary accepting something she couldn't understand—it's all so human.

Any time that God interrupts our lives in a supernatural way, it's a lot to take in. Supernatural interruptions happen today, too, and when the story is yours, it feels no less dramatic than the ones we read in the Bible. Faith is not easy for any generation. But always, stepping out and believing God's promises is how our best stories begin.

ALL POINTS *West*

"We saw His star in the east and have come to worship Him" (Matthew 2:2).

Magi FROM THE *east* ARRIVED IN JERUSALEM, SAYING, "*Where is He*

WHO HAS BEEN BORN *King of the Jews*? FOR WE SAW *His star* IN THE EAST

AND HAVE COME TO *worship* HIM." —MATTHEW 2:1–2

STAR OF WONDER, STAR OF NIGHT

A STAR SHONE BRIGHTLY IN THE HEAVENS—*His star.* The wise men, or *magi*, who saw it knew they had to follow.

How did they know? What compelled them to undertake this arduous journey toward the unknown? What *was* it about that star?

Hailing from Babylon—or very near it—the magi would have been familiar with the stories of the biblical prophet Daniel, who had been appointed in his day as "chief of the magicians." Daniel's teachings and the biblical writings his people brought into exile, including those on the hope for a kingly Messiah, would have been passed down through generations of wise men.

Noting an unusual stellar phenomenon in the sky, the magi drew on their knowledge of astronomy and biblical revelation, likely recalling Balaam's prophecy:

> "A star shall come forth from Jacob,
> A scepter shall rise from Israel."

So convinced were they that they packed treasures and followed the mysterious star to the capital city of Israel, Jerusalem, ready to worship the King of the Jews. Once they arrived, a troubled King Herod inquired of the Jewish religious leaders and determined that, according to Hebrew prophecy, the King would be born in the town of Bethlehem (Micah 5:2). Having Herod's supposed blessing, the magi continued their journey. The star, absent during their brief sojourn in Jerusalem, reappeared, leading these wise men to rejoice "exceedingly with great joy."

Their reaction to the star's reappearance—*joy!*—as well as to the Child—*worship!*—shows the humility of these learned men. They understood who Jesus was . . . the King for all to worship. As they bowed down before the Child, these men of the nations anticipated a glorious future, when every knee shall bow and every tongue confess that Jesus is Lord (Philippians 2:10–11).

A desire to see the King compelled them to come. An eye on the stars directed their path. A sense of wonder caused them to drop to their knees in worship. The journey of the magi from Babylon to Bethlehem, led by hope and a star, adds a remarkable chapter to the coming of God in human flesh.

See Numbers 24:17; Daniel 4:9; and Matthew 2:1–12.

We often picture the magi bowing before baby Jesus in the manger, but was that the case? When the magi visited Jesus, He was more child than infant, a fact indicated by Matthew's word choice. He used the word paidion, *meaning "child" (Matthew 2:9, 11), while Luke, in his account of Jesus's birth, used the word* brephos, *which means "infant" (Luke 2:12, 16). The magi also visited Jesus in a house, so some time had to have passed between His birth and the magi's visit. In fact, the book of Matthew implies that Jesus would have been about two years old at this time (Matthew 2:16).*

AFTER COMING INTO THE HOUSE

THEY SAW THE *Child*

WITH MARY HIS MOTHER;

AND THEY FELL TO THE GROUND

AND *worshiped Him.*

THEN, OPENING THEIR TREASURES,

THEY PRESENTED TO HIM

GIFTS OF *gold, frankincense,*

AND *myrrh.*

—MATTHEW 2:11

*Frankincense was burned in the
temple for its fragrant aroma.*

BRING HIM INCENSE, GOLD, AND MYRRH

WHAT DO YOU GIVE a young king? The magi, after traveling more than five hundred miles away to see the child Jesus, brought gold, frankincense, and myrrh with them. Why those gifts? What did the gifts mean in relation to Jesus? And what did they mean for the men who gave them?

Gold. The magi, even before they arrived at Jesus's home, knew they were searching for a king. As men who acknowledged Jesus as sovereign ruler, they brought a gift befitting someone of rank and authority. Gold has long been used as a medium of exchange—whether as coins or as the basis of the value of a coin. In gold, the magi brought a gift of great value, a symbol of sacrifice on their part as worshipers. Gold represented their willingness to give everything to God, because He alone is worthy.

Frankincense. Worshipers in the Old Testament inserted the dried gum of frankincense into candles to make offerings in the temple. The frankincense candles released a fragrant scent that filled the room with an exquisite aroma. That the magi brought frankincense to Jesus demonstrates that they acknowledged the Child not simply as King but also as Priest who would intercede for humanity before God. In this way, the frankincense was a symbol of the magi's humility before the Child, recognizing their dependence on a holy and just God.

Myrrh. The ancients used myrrh when embalming the dead, making the gift especially appropriate for Jesus, whose death would change history. While the magi likely had no concept of the death Jesus would die, the gift signified the importance of Jesus's death. In fact, when Joseph of Arimathea and Nicodemus took Jesus from the cross and prepared His body for the tomb, they used a mixture of aloe and myrrh. The gummy consistency of that mixture would help hold together the cloth wrappings that surrounded the body.

The King received the gold. Our Intercessor took the frankincense. And the One who died on the cross had myrrh wrapped about His body by His friends. The magi's gifts to Jesus pointed to the utterly unique, glorious, and sacrificial ministry of the Lord Jesus.[1]

See Matthew 2:11–12 and John 19:38–40.

Everyone knows what gold is, but what exactly are frankincense and myrrh? Frankincense comes from the resin of the boswellia tree. Cut into the wood with a sharp knife and out bleeds an amber-colored oil that eventually dries into a thick, gummy substance. Myrrh was a resin extracted from a variety of trees in the Middle East, collected by slicing the tree and catching the oily substance in a small, square, wooden collecting basin.

Behold, AN ANGEL OF THE LORD APPEARED TO JOSEPH IN A DREAM AND SAID, "*Get up!*

TAKE THE CHILD AND HIS MOTHER AND *flee to Egypt*, AND REMAIN THERE UNTIL I TELL YOU;

FOR *Herod* IS GOING TO SEARCH FOR THE *Child* TO *destroy* HIM." —MATTHEW 2:13

JOSEPH, LEND YOUR AID

GET UP!

Joseph sat up in bed, the words still ringing in his ears. His eyes darted back and forth looking for the source of that voice. His room lay dark, the gentle breathing of his wife and child filling the space.

As his haze cleared, Joseph began to think back through his dream. Was it true? Did God really want him to take his family out of Israel and into Egypt? He considered for only a moment. Of course it was true. The message was so clear. He had not been as convinced of anything since that earlier dream, when the angel told him to take Mary as his wife despite her pregnancy (Matthew 1:18–25).

Joseph turned and woke his wife. As he repeated the dream to her, the desperation of their situation began to set in. If they didn't take quick action, Herod's men would, within a matter of days or even hours, rip the beautiful Child from their arms and kill Him before their eyes. They had to move *now*.

As Mary prepared a few things inside the home, Joseph stepped out to their small stable and prepared their donkey. With just a few items on their backs, a little food, some money for the journey, and the Child in tow, the family began the long journey south, down the Hebron road bound for Egypt.

Up to this point, Joseph had been in a difficult position for a father. With Mary the chosen mother of God's Son and the Child's redemptive task in human history, Joseph's role seemed limited in comparison. *What can I do?* he may have wondered. Sure, he worked for the family and provided a home, clothing, and shelter, but this was what any other father would do for his family.

Joseph, Mary, and Jesus traveled the International Highway, an ancient trade route to Egypt.

With the message from the angel, however, Joseph took on a special role. The Lord's message prompted Joseph to take responsibility for his family and save them from the evil devices of Herod. And Joseph, during a critical moment both in his life and in human history, made the right choice. Just as he did when the angel told him to take Mary as his wife, Joseph jumped up from a dead sleep in obedience to an arduous command from God.

See Matthew 2:13–15.

When Joseph led his wife and child out of Israel and into Egypt, the event was evocative of Israel's sojourn in Egypt some fifteen hundred years earlier. In both cases, a man named Joseph brought his people to Egypt for their protection and benefit. And in both instances, the return to Israel served as an example of God keeping His promises (Genesis 12:1; 15:13; Hosea 11:1).

The Herodium, a man-made mountain-fortress and Herod the Great's palace, still overlooks the town of Bethlehem.

WHEN *Herod* SAW THAT HE HAD BEEN TRICKED BY THE MAGI, HE BECAME *very enraged*,

AND SENT AND *slew* ALL THE *male children* WHO WERE IN BETHLEHEM

AND ALL ITS VICINITY, FROM TWO YEARS OLD AND UNDER. —MATTHEW 2:16

HEROD THE KING, IN HIS RAGING

HISTORY HAS CONFERRED THE TITLE "THE GREAT" to King Herod's name due to the extraordinary building projects he undertook. Herod constructed Israel's first man-made port in Caesarea, a grand winter palace in Jericho and, his crowning achievement, the temple in Jerusalem.

But this great king also suffered from paranoia that his Jewish subjects would revolt or that his own family members would plot his assassination. So, Herod simply executed those he saw as a threat. Problem solved!

Because of his incessant suspicions, Herod built or rebuilt eleven fortresses across Israel—places he could escape to at a moment's notice. The three most significant strongholds stood in Jerusalem, at Masada, and at a site he named after himself—the Herodium.

The wise magi from the east had journeyed to Jerusalem and inquired of King Herod, "Where is He who has been born King of the Jews?" A naive question from such wise men! For Herod to hear that another king had been born was all the incentive he needed to search for and murder the young boy. But Joseph, Mary, and Jesus already were safely escaping to Egypt. Herod slaughtered all boys in Bethlehem two years old and younger, but he did not succeed in his mission to kill the King of the Jews.

Years later, the raging King Herod died and was buried in the Herodium, where archaeologists recently have discovered his tomb. The Herodium site, now in ruins, still overlooks nearby Bethlehem—ironically, the birthplace of the true King of Israel.

Herod "slew all the male children who were in Bethlehem . . . from two years old and under" (Matthew 2:16).

More than three decades after Herod's death, on Jesus's final journey up to Jerusalem, He walked between the buildings of Herod's palace in Jericho. As the shadows of the opulent buildings fell upon the Savior, He must have considered this obsessed king who tried to kill Him as a boy. Ironically, King Herod died in the Jericho palace while King Jesus lived to pass between its walls . . . on His way to willingly lay down *His* life for all sins.

Today, each of Herod the Great's ornate palaces and fortresses lies in ruins—a testimony to all earthly glory.

See Matthew 2:2, 16–18.

Almost two thousand years before Joseph and Mary journeyed to Bethlehem, Jacob and Rachel, another expectant couple, traveled the same road. Rachel gave birth to Benjamin, but she died after delivery, and Jacob buried her near Bethlehem (Genesis 35:19). Rachel's death foreshadowed the devastation that the territory of Benjamin suffered in Jeremiah's time, as the prophet wrote:

> *"Rachel is weeping for her children . . .*
> *Because they are no more." (Jeremiah 31:15)*

The cryptic prophecy found its final fulfillment in Jesus's time, when Herod the Great slaughtered all baby boys in Bethlehem (Matthew 2:16–18). (Modern Bethlehem pictured above.)

THE *Story* CONTINUES . . .

But [He] *emptied Himself,*

TAKING THE FORM OF A BOND-SERVANT,

AND *being made in the likeness of men.* —PHILIPPIANS 2:7

I Heard the Bells on Christmas Day

THERE ONCE LIVED A FARMER who became jaded about Christmas and all things "Christian."

Late one raw winter night, he sat alone in the house, reading. In the quiet he heard an irregular thumping against the back porch door. He flipped  on the light. To his surprise, the birds that had made their nests in a nearby tree were flying against the glass, almost as if knocking to come inside. The limb on which they had built their nest had fallen under the weight of the ice. His heart went out to them.

He pulled on his snow boots and overcoat and pushed open the storm door. Immediately the birds fluttered away. Against knee-deep snow, he made his way out to the barn. He slid open the barn door and wondered how he could get the frightened birds into its warmth and safety.

He built a massive nest out of hay, but they wouldn't come near. He sprinkled some crackers in a path from their tree toward the barn. But they didn't follow. He tried to shoo them in, but they only scattered. He even lit a couple of candles inside the barn, hoping the added warmth would draw them. But to the birds, he was only something to be afraid of. He knew nothing of their language and nothing of their world.

He thought, *If there were just some way that I could become a bird. If only for a few moments I could communicate to them how much I care, I could get them into the barn and they would be safe and warm.*

At that moment, as only God would plan it, church bells began to ring in the distance. The farmer suddenly remembered, as he looked at his watch and checked the date, that it was Christmas morning.

At that moment, he grasped the true meaning of Christmas. A man becoming a bird is nothing compared to God's becoming a man. This was what *the Savior* did—He came to rescue the farmer himself and all humanity from the cold of sin. There in the deep snow on the back porch he fell to his knees, softened his heart, and returned to the Lord his God.[1]

See Philippians 2:6–11.

During the Christmas season when so much emphasis is on the wrong things, when the minors seem to get the major emphasis, and the simple significance of a baby born to a Jewish couple in Bethlehem gets lost somehow in the shuffle of activities, take time to pause. Take a walk in the snow if you have some. Listen to the Christmas bells ring, breathe a prayer of thanks, and remember, "a Savior is born." O come, let us adore Him.

"MEN OF GALILEE, WHY DO YOU STAND LOOKING INTO THE SKY?

THIS *Jesus*, WHO HAS BEEN *taken up* FROM YOU INTO HEAVEN,

WILL *come* IN JUST THE *same way* AS

YOU HAVE WATCHED HIM GO INTO HEAVEN."   —ACTS 1:11

Suddenly the Lord, Descending

JESUS HAS COME. And Jesus is coming again.

Before the nativity, before Jesus took on flesh as holy Child, God's people waited, hoping that He would one day come and deliver them. They studied and believed and passed on to future generations the promises of God's Word. These promises extend all the way back to the first moments after Adam and Eve fell into sin (Genesis 3:14–15), and they stretch across all of Old Testament revelation (Malachi 3:1; 4:5–6).

Armed with the promise of eternal salvation and with the faith that God had delivered in the past, the faithful few hoped in the coming Messiah. No special signs were given to alert them to His coming. No special calendar could be devised to discover the date of His arrival. They had only God's Word and a simple, fervent trust that He was faithful to bring it to pass.

And then finally He was with them. God had sent the Deliverer, an answer to their hopes, a fulfillment to His promises. Jesus was formed in the womb of a virgin, born in Bethlehem, and called out from Egypt. God orchestrated all the details and brought each of His assurances to pass. The faithful few had their trust rewarded. They rejoiced at Jesus's arrival, gloried in His miracles, and trusted in His death and resurrection.

But then He left. Here for a few decades, then gone, leaving only a pledge of His return. The angels who attended His ascension spoke the promise to the few followers present, "This Jesus, who has been taken up from you into heaven, will come in just the same way as you have watched Him go into heaven."

"As [Jesus] was sitting on the Mount of Olives, the disciples came to Him privately, saying, 'Tell us, when will these things happen, and what will be the sign of Your coming . . . ?'" (Matthew 24:3).

For nearly two thousand years since, Christians have found themselves in much the same position as those Old Testament saints. We have waited, and we have wondered, *When will He come?* No calendar will reveal the date; no sign will alert us to His coming. When He comes, He will come unannounced. But He will come. That is our hope. And we know it will be fulfilled because He came before.

Jesus has come. And Jesus will come again. Come quickly, Lord Jesus!

See Acts 1:9–11.

Christians have the hope that Jesus will come again for His church just before the end of time. We call this the rapture, *which will occur just before the tribulation—when God will bring judgment for sin to the earth. Afterward, Jesus will descend to earth, coming a second time, and He will rule over an eternal kingdom.*

63

How to Begin a *Relationship* with *God*

Since Adam and Eve sinned in the garden of Eden, human beings have experienced seasons of feeling distant from God. In those times, we picture Him in some remote place, far from the concerns of His creation. And we wonder: *Does God still care for us? Does He still desire a relationship with human beings?*

When God's Son came to earth, born as an infant in human flesh, the Lord made His loudest declaration to all humanity that *yes* He loves us and desires our love in return. Through sin, we separated ourselves from God. But rather than let us wallow alone, God took the initiative and came near to us in His Son, Jesus. If you're interested in beginning a relationship with God, the Bible marks the path with four essential truths. Let's look at each marker in detail.

Our Spiritual Condition: Totally Depraved

The first truth is rather personal. One look in the mirror of Scripture, and our human condition becomes painfully clear:

> "There is none righteous, not even one;
> There is none who understands,
> There is none who seeks for God;
> All have turned aside, together they have become useless;
> There is none who does good,
> There is not even one." (Romans 3:10–12)

We are all sinners through and through—totally depraved. Now, that doesn't mean we've committed every atrocity known to humankind. We're not as *bad* as we can be, just as *bad off* as we can be. Sin colors all our thoughts, motives, words, and actions.

If you've been around a while, you likely already believe it. Look around. Everything around us bears the smudge marks of our sinful nature. Despite our best efforts to create a perfect world, crime statistics continue to soar, divorce rates keep climbing, and families keep crumbling.

Something has gone terribly wrong in our society and in ourselves—something deadly. Contrary to how the world would repackage it, "me-first" living doesn't equal rugged individuality and freedom; it equals death. As Paul said in his letter to the Romans, "The wages of sin is death" (Romans 6:23)—our spiritual and physical death that comes from God's righteous judgment of our sin, along with all of the emotional and practical effects of this separation that we experience on a daily basis. This brings us to the second marker: God's character.

God's Character: Infinitely Holy

How can God judge us for a sinful state we were born into? Our total depravity is only half the answer. The other half is God's infinite holiness.

The fact that we know things are not as they should be points us to a standard of goodness beyond ourselves. Our sense of injustice in life on this side of eternity implies a perfect standard of justice beyond our reality. That standard and source is God Himself. And God's standard of holiness contrasts starkly with our sinful condition.

Scripture says that "God is Light, and in Him there is no darkness at all" (1 John 1:5). God is absolutely holy—which creates a problem for us. If He is so pure, how can we who are so impure relate to Him?

Perhaps we could try being better people, try to tilt the balance in favor of our good deeds, or seek out methods for self-improvement. Throughout history, people have attempted to live up to God's standard by keeping the Ten Commandments or living by their own code of ethics. Unfortunately, no one can come close to satisfying the demands of God's law. Romans 3:20 says, "By the works of the Law no flesh will be justified in His sight; for through the Law comes the knowledge of sin."

Our Need: A Substitute

So here we are, sinners by nature and sinners by choice, trying to pull ourselves up by our own bootstraps to attain a relationship with our holy Creator. But every time we try, we fall flat on our faces. We can't live a good enough life to make up for our sin, because God's standard isn't "good enough"—it's *perfection*. And we can't make amends for the offense our sin has created without dying for it.

Who can get us out of this mess?

If someone could live perfectly, honoring God's law, and would bear sin's death penalty for us—in our place—then we would be saved from our predicament. But is there such a person? Thankfully, yes!

Meet your substitute—*Jesus Christ.* He is the One who took death's place for you!

> [God] made [Jesus Christ] who knew no sin to be sin on our behalf, so that we might become the righteousness of God in Him. (2 Corinthians 5:21)

God's Provision: A Savior

God rescued us by sending His Son, Jesus, to die on the cross for our sins (1 John 4:9–10). Jesus was fully human and fully divine (John 1:1, 18), a truth that ensures His understanding of our weaknesses, His power to forgive, and His ability to bridge the gap between God and us (Romans 5:6–11). In short, we are "justified as a gift by His grace through the redemption which is in Christ Jesus" (Romans 3:24). Two words in this verse bear further explanation: *justified* and *redemption.*

Justification is God's act of mercy, in which He declares righteous the believing sinners while we are still in our sinning state. Justification doesn't mean that God *makes* us righteous, so that we never sin again, rather that He *declares* us righteous—much like a judge pardons a guilty criminal. Because Jesus took our sin upon Himself and suffered our judgment on the cross, God forgives our debt and proclaims us PARDONED.

Redemption is Christ's act of paying the complete price to release us from sin's bondage. God sent His Son to bear His wrath for all of our sins—past, present, and future (Romans 3:24–26; 2 Corinthians 5:21). In humble obedience, Christ willingly endured the shame of the cross for our sake (Mark 10:45; Romans 5:6–8; Philippians 2:8). Christ's death satisfied God's righteous demands. He no longer holds our sins against us, because His own Son paid the penalty for them. We are freed from the slave market of sin, never to be enslaved again!

Placing Your Faith in Christ

These four truths describe how God has provided a way to Himself through Jesus Christ. Because the price has been paid in full by God, we must respond to His free gift of eternal life in total faith and confidence in Him to save us. We must step forward into the relationship with God that He has prepared for us—not by doing good works or by being a good person but by coming to Him just as we are and accepting His justification and redemption by faith.

> For by grace you have been saved through faith; and that not of yourselves, it is the gift of God; not as a result of works, so that no one may boast. (Ephesians 2:8–9)

We accept God's gift of salvation simply by placing our faith in Christ alone for the forgiveness of our sins. Would you like to enter a relationship with your Creator by trusting in Christ as your Savior? If so, here's a simple prayer you can use to express your faith:

> *Dear God,*
>
> *I know that my sin has put a barrier between You and me. Thank You for sending Your Son, Jesus, to die in my place. I trust in Jesus alone to forgive my sins, and I accept His gift of eternal life. I ask Jesus to be my personal Savior and the Lord of my life. Thank You. In Jesus's name, amen.*

If you've prayed this prayer or one like it and you wish to find out more about knowing God and His plan for you in the Bible, contact us at Insight for Living Ministries. Our contact information is on the following pages.

WE ARE HERE *for You*

If you desire to find out more about knowing God and His plan for you in the Bible, contact us. Insight for Living Ministries provides staff pastors who are available for free written correspondence or phone consultation. These seminary-trained and seasoned counselors have years of experience and are well-qualified guides for your spiritual journey.

Please feel welcome to contact your regional office by using the information below:

United States
Insight for Living Ministries
Biblical Counseling Department
Post Office Box 5000
Frisco, Texas 75034-0055
USA
469-535-8397
(Monday through Friday,
8:00 a.m.–5:00 p.m. central time)
www.insight.org/contactapastor

Canada
Insight for Living Canada
Biblical Counseling Department
PO Box 8 Stn A
Abbotsford BC V2T 6Z4
CANADA
1-800-663-7639
info@insightforliving.ca

Australia, New Zealand, and South Pacific
Insight for Living Australia
Pastoral Care
Post Office Box 443
Boronia, VIC 3155
AUSTRALIA
+61 3 9762 6613

United Kingdom and Europe
Insight for Living United Kingdom
Pastoral Care
PO Box 553
Dorking
RH4 9EU
UNITED KINGDOM
0800 787 9364
+44 1306 640156
www.insightforliving.org.uk

Ordering INFORMATION

If you would like to order additional copies of *A Promise Kept: A Pictorial Journey of the Coming of Christ* or other Insight for Living Ministries resources, please contact the office that serves you.

United States
Insight for Living Ministries
Post Office Box 5000
Frisco, Texas 75034-0055
USA
1-800-772-8888
(Monday through Friday,
7:00 a.m.–7:00 p.m. central time)
www.insight.org
www.insightworld.org

Canada
Insight for Living Canada
PO Box 8 Stn A
Abbotsford BC V2T 6Z4
CANADA
1-800-663-7639
www.insightforliving.ca

Australia, New Zealand, and South Pacific
Insight for Living Australia
Post Office Box 443
Boronia, VIC 3155
AUSTRALIA
+61 3 9762 6613
www.ifl.org.au

United Kingdom and Europe
Insight for Living United Kingdom
PO Box 553
Dorking
RH4 9EU
UNITED KINGDOM
0800 787 9364
+44 1306 640156
www.insightforliving.org.uk

Other International Locations
International constituents
may contact the U.S. office
through our Web site
(www.insightworld.org),
mail queries, or by calling
+1-469-535-8436.

Questions FOR FAMILY TALKS AND GROUP DISCUSSIONS

Watching Long in Hope and Fear, devotion on page 7.
Read Mark 1:1–3.

Between the Old and New Testaments, there were four hundred years when no one spoke on God's behalf. God wasn't showing up anywhere to humanity. God's people knew He had promised a Messiah—but all they could do was wait.

1. Name some things for which you have waited. How long have you waited?

2. What are common temptations that you might think of or feel as you wait?

3. What was happening four hundred years ago in your country's history? Doesn't that seem like a long time ago? Now imagine that's how long Israel had waited for a Messiah. What do you imagine the people were tempted to think?

4. Read Romans 8:28. In what ways have you seen or now see God orchestrating the events of your life . . . for His glory and your good?

Late in Time Behold Him Come, devotion on page 9.
Read Galatians 4:4.

God's choice of timing and location are always perfect.

1. Just imagine if Jesus were born today in your town, rather than in Bethlehem at the beginning of the first century. Where might He be born? What would the angels say? Who would play the role of shepherds?

2. Do you believe God is in charge of history? Do you think anything surprises Him or delays His purposes? Do you think God's will is always accomplished?

Pleased as Man with Men to Dwell, devotion on page 13.
Read Luke 1:26–27.

Little is secret when you grow up in a small town or any close-knit community. For better or worse, you know people and they know you.

1. As Jesus grew up, how do you think God used the climate of Jesus's hometown to prepare Him for ministry?

2. Do you know what it's like to come from a hometown with a bad reputation? How does it shape your character?

3. Do you ever question God's wisdom when He uses unexpected or undesirable people to accomplish His plan? Do you ever wonder why He wants to use you?

The Angel Gabriel from Heaven Came, devotion on page 15.
Read Luke 1:12–13.

Angels are just downright interesting. The fact that there's a whole other world happening around us that we can't see is both exciting and a bit unsettling.

1. How does it make you feel to know that angels are living in a world around you — even though you can't see them?

2. What do you find comforting or challenging about what we know of the activities in the supernatural world?

His Gospel Is Peace, devotion on page 17.
Read Luke 1:5–20.

On the biggest day of his life—the biggest day of his career—Zacharias was surprised by an angel who told him something he didn't believe . . . and consequences followed.

1. What would your daily life be like if you couldn't speak a word? How would you communicate? What do you think you would learn?

2. Have you found it difficult to believe any of God's promises? Which ones? How do you counter doubt with truth?

Pierce the Clouds and Bring Us Light, devotion on page 19.
Read Luke 1:24–58.

Elizabeth had waited a long, long time for God to give her and her husband a baby. Imagine how surprised she was to hear—from an angel!—that she was going to be a mother.

1. Elizabeth was probably close to the age of a grandmother when she was told she was going to have a baby. *Too old*, some would say. Why do you think she made a really good mom for John the Baptist?

2. Elizabeth recognized that God had "looked with favor" on her. What does "God's favor" mean to you?

Mary Was That Mother Mild, devotion on page 21.
Read Luke 1:26–38.

An ordinary day for Mary turned out to be the turning point of her whole life.

1. Mary had to set aside her own plans for the future to do what God had planned for her. What character choices does it take to surrender your own plans in order to follow God's plans?

2. In Mary's song and prayer in Luke 1:46–55, she gave evidence that she knew the promises of God very well and even had a lot of Scripture memorized. Do you know any Scripture by heart? What would you like to memorize and remember during life's important moments?

Joseph Dearest, Joseph Mine, devotion on page 23.
Read Matthew 1:20–25.

Sometimes life doesn't go as planned. This is what Mary and Joseph faced when their customary wedding plans changed (significantly!).

1. How do you think Joseph felt when Mary told him about the baby?

2. Why is it important to believe what God says rather than believe what we feel?

3. What character traits do you see evident in Joseph's response to the original challenge, to the angel's direction, and to Mary?

4. Why might some call Joseph "the hero behind the scenes"?

Jesus, Our Emmanuel, devotion on page 25.
Read Isaiah 9:6.

Not only was Jesus a baby born in a manger in Bethlehem, but Jesus is also the Son of God, who has always existed—even before time began. Humanity's story contains whispers of Jesus that show up in every book of the Bible.

1. From the Old Testament books, what is your favorite picture of Jesus? As the Passover Lamb in Exodus? As the Shepherd in Psalm 23? As the Prince of Peace in the writings of the prophets?

2. What New Testament promise do you most appreciate?

3. Pick one of the descriptions listed in this devotional and describe further to someone what Jesus means to you.

O Come, Thou Key of David, Come, devotion on page 27.
Read Galatians 4:4.

When you look closely at history with eyes of faith, it's clear that God has always had a plan.

1. How much of your family's history do you know? What are your grandparents' names? Where were they born?

2. Why is it important that Jesus is in the lineage of King David?

3. How does Jesus's "family tree" bolster your confidence that God keeps His promises?

Sovereign Father, Heavenly King, devotion on page 29.
Read Hebrews 11:1.

Unless you happened to be in the Bethlehem fields and saw the angels announcing Jesus's birth, you wouldn't have realized that something big happened that night.

1. What people think is important and what God thinks is important are sometimes flipped upside down. What is something that people put a high priority on but God doesn't? What is something that God values highly, yet people don't? How does this perspective influence your priorities?

2. When life's circumstances are hard, it's easy to forget God's promises. How would you fill in this statement: In spite of _____, I believe God will _____.

O Little Town of Bethlehem, devotion on page 33.
Read Luke 2:5–7.

Every Christmas, we likely hear the carol "O Little Town of Bethlehem." Bethlehem is a real place.

1. Look at some of the Christmas cards your family has received. What are some common pictures on each of the cards? Do you think you would have recognized Jesus as "something special," or did He look like any other baby boy?

2. Too often we expect God to show up in our lives in loud and showy ways, when He more often chooses to speak through humble people and quiet circumstances. The circumstances surrounding Jesus's birth are a perfect example. Can you recall times when God showed up in your life in an unexpected way or through an unexpected person?

Offspring of the Virgin's Womb, devotion on page 35.
Read Isaiah 7:14 and Matthew 1:18−25.

The Christmas miracle happened nine months before Jesus was born. God put life in Mary's womb! What normally happens when a man and a woman make a baby, God did without human interaction at all!

1. Think about Jesus's conception from Mary and Joseph's perspective: they knew without a doubt that Mary was a virgin, and yet now they were told she was pregnant! Do you think they understood what a big deal this was?

2. Think about Jesus's conception from Jesus's perspective: since before time, Jesus knew this day would come. How do you imagine He anticipated "taking on flesh" and becoming a man with limitations?

The Wonder of It All, devotion on page 37.
Read Luke 2.

Even though it was one of the greatest nights in history, the night Jesus was born was as ordinary as today.

1. How might have Mary and Joseph comforted each other during the stressful hours of labor in such humble surroundings away from family and loved ones?

2. What do you think Mary and Joseph's fears and concerns were as they cared for newborn Jesus?

Mary, Did You Know? devotion on page 39.
Read Luke 1:26−56.

Mary was an ordinary girl in an extraordinary situation.

1. Which of the questions stated in this lesson made you pause and wonder about her answer?

2. Think of three of your own questions for Mary.

To Certain Poor Shepherds, devotion on page 41.
Read Luke 2:11−12.

Picture the shepherds going about their tasks as usual when the night sky split open and countless brightly shining beings filled the darkness.

1. How would you react if you were surprised like that?

2. Why do you think God chose to announce Jesus's birth . . . to shepherds (a very small, disrespected pocket of society)?

Hail the Incarnate Deity, devotion on page 43.
Read Philippians 2:5−8 and John 1:14.

It's hard to think about Jesus being alive before He came to earth as a baby, but the Bible tells us that Jesus always existed as a Person of the Trinity (another difficult concept to understand that we believe by faith).

1. Philippians 2:5−8 gives us a snapshot of Jesus's decision to come to earth as a baby. He did it by choice in obedience to His Father's instructions. Do you think this was a difficult decision?

2. This section of the Bible points us to Jesus's humility. How would you define *humility*? What did it look like in Jesus's life? What does it look like in the lives of people you admire? What does it look like in your life? Give examples of what a humble person does or what he or she thinks.

The Hopes and Fears of All the Years, devotion on page 45.
Read Luke 2:25−35.

We're not told how long Simeon waited for God to fulfill His promise that Simeon would not die before he saw the Messiah. We can guess that he waited a long time—perhaps years, even decades.

1. What's the longest you've waited for something?

2. What do you think were some of the feelings that Simeon had when he held the Messiah? What did their interaction with Simeon do for Mary and Joseph's faith?

Like Mary, Let Us Ponder, devotion on page 47.
Read Luke 2:19, 51.

Mary and Joseph were people just like us. Remember that as you read the Christmas story.

1. How do you think Mary felt to be chosen for such an amazing responsibility?

2. How does knowing that Luke 1 and 2 were influenced by Mary's memories personalize the account for you?

3. As you look back on your life with the perspective of years gone by, do you see God's hand at work in ways other than those you recognized as you were experiencing the circumstances?

Star of Wonder, Star of Night, devotion on page 51.
Read Numbers 24:17 and Matthew 2:1–12.

On a clear night, go outside and look at the stars. Psalm 19:1 says "the heavens are telling of the glory of God." God also uses His creation for special communication.

1. The star was a special phenomenon that God provided for a special time in history. What does this miracle say about God's desire that Jesus's birth be known to the world?

2. A popular bumper sticker says, "Wise Men Still Seek Him." What does this mean to you?

Bring Him Incense, Gold, and Myrrh, devotion on page 53.
Read Matthew 2:11–12.

Every chapter of human history reveals people who have been seekers of truth. God promises that those who seek Him will find Him when they search for Him with all their hearts (Jeremiah 29:13).

1. How do the gifts that the magi gave to Joseph reflect the magi's understanding of who Jesus really was?

   Gold:

   Frankincense:

   Myrrh:

2. Practically speaking, how might these gifts have been a provision from the Lord for the emergency trip Joseph and his family took to Egypt?

Joseph, Lend Your Aid, devotion on page 55.
Read Matthew 2:13–15.

Consider the time Jesus left the land of Israel when He was a baby, when Joseph and Mary escaped Herod's murderous plot.

1. How did Joseph act like a father in this scary situation?

2. How did Mary act like a wife in this scary situation?

Herod the King, in His Raging, devotion on page 57.
Read Matthew 2:16–18.

Right in the middle of the wonderful Christmas story came a slap back to reality. A madman was on the loose— and he ruled that small world with a paranoid, murderous hand.

1. If you were Joseph and Mary, how would you feel when you heard about Herod's intent to kill your son? What would you do?

2. What harm did Herod think Jesus was going to do to him?

I Heard the Bells on Christmas Day, devotion on page 61.
Read Philippians 2:7.

Sometimes stories help us jump between a hard-to-understand idea and what that idea really means.

1. Do you know anyone like the cranky farmer who didn't want anything to do with Christmas?

2. Why did the farmer want the birds to go into the barn?

Suddenly the Lord, Descending, devotion on page 63.
Read Acts 1:9–11.

Now that we've read a part of the story—a very exciting beginning chapter of the earthly life of Jesus who was born a baby, who grew up to be a man, the Messiah who came to die for the sins of the world—are you ready for more? This true story is only the beginning!

1. Like the people who had only God's Word and a promise from God, what are you trusting God to do for you?

2. Are you ready for Jesus's return? Perhaps today He will call us to join Him in the clouds!

Endnotes

NAZARETH

1. The historical facts and interpretation are from Ronald B. Allen, "Does Anything Good Come from Nazareth?" *Kindred Spirit* 23, no. 4 (1999), http://www.dts.edu/publications/read/does-anything-good-come-from-nazareth-ronald-b-allen (accessed July 20, 2010).

2. Adapted from Charles R. Swindoll, "Meet Gabriel . . . the Heaven-Sent Angel," in *A Bethlehem Christmas*, message series (2007), and from "The Day Mary Met Gabriel," in *The Origination of Something Glorious*, message series (1992).

3. Frederick William Danker, ed., *A Greek-English Lexicon of the New Testament and Other Early Christian Literature,* rev. 3d. ed. (Chicago: University of Chicago Press, 2000), 199.

4. Adapted from Charles R. Swindoll, *Jesus: The Greatest Life of All* (Nashville: Thomas Nelson, 2008), 17–29; and from Charles R. Swindoll, "A Birth," in *Growing Strong in the Seasons of Life* (Portland, Ore.: Multnomah, 1983), 49.

BETHLEHEM

1. Lyrics by Phillips Brooks, "O Little Town of Bethlehem"; devotional adapted from Wayne Stiles, *Going Places with God: A Devotional Journey through the Lands of the Bible* (Ventura, Calif.: Regal, 2006), 130. Used by permission.

2. Adapted from Charles R. Swindoll, "Mary, Mother of Jesus," in *The Wise and the Wild: 30 Devotions on Women of the Bible* (Plano, Tex.: Insight for Living, 2010), 75–76.

3. Adapted from Wayne Stiles, *Walking in the Footsteps of Jesus: A Journey Through the Lands and Lessons of Christ* (Ventura, Calif.: Regal, 2008), 18–19. Used by permission.

4. Adapted from Charles R. Swindoll, "Meet Immanuel . . . the Indescribable Gift," in *A Bethlehem Christmas*, message series (2007).

ALL POINTS WEST

1. Adapted from Charles R. Swindoll, "Lord, My Gift to You Is _____," in *Holiday Messages*, message series (December 18, 1996–January 3, 1997).

THE STORY CONTINUES . . .

1. Adapted from a story by Philip Yancey and Paul Harvey, as retold by Charles R. Swindoll, in *Come Before Winter and Share My Hope* (Grand Rapids: Zondervan, 1985), 351–52.

Carol and Hymn Titles

O Come, Let Us Adore Him, Christ the Lord from *O Come, All Ye Faithful*; **Watching Long in Hope and Fear** from *Angels, from the Realms of Glory*; **Late in Time Behold Him Come** from *Hark! the Herald Angels Sing*; **Pleased as Man with Men to Dwell** from *Hark! the Herald Angels Sing*; **The Angel Gabriel from Heaven Came** from *Gabriel's Message*; **His Gospel Is Peace** from *Silent Night! Holy Night!*; **Pierce the Clouds and Bring Us Light** from *O Come, O Come, Emmanuel*; **Mary Was That Mother Mild** from *Once in Royal David's City*; **Joseph Dearest, Joseph Mine** from *Joseph Dearest, Joseph Mine*; **Jesus, Our Emmanuel** from *Hark! the Herald Angels Sing*; **O Come, Thou Key of David, Come** from *O Come, O Come, Emmanuel*; **Sovereign Father, Heavenly King** from *Glory Be to God on High*; **O Little Town of Bethlehem** from *O Little Town of Bethlehem*; **Offspring of the Virgin's Womb** from *Hark! the Herald Angels Sing*; **The Wonder of It All** from *The Wonder of It All*; **Mary, Did You Know?** from *Mary, Did You Know?*; **To Certain Poor Shepherds** from *The First Noel*; **Hail the Incarnate Deity** from *Hark! the Herald Angels Sing*; **The Hopes and Fears of All the Years** from *O Little Town of Bethlehem*; **Like Mary, Let Us Ponder** from *Christians, Awake, Salute the Happy Morn*; **Star of Wonder, Star of Night** from *We Three Kings*; **Bring Him Incense, Gold, and Myrrh** from *What Child Is This?*; **Joseph, Lend Your Aid** from *Angels We Have Heard on High* ; **Herod the King, in His Raging** from *Coventry Carol*; **I Heard the Bells on Christmas Day** from *I Heard the Bells on Christmas Day*; **Suddenly the Lord, Descending** from *Angels, from the Realms of Glory*

Copyrights

A Promise Kept
A Pictorial Journey of the Coming of Christ

From the Bible-Teaching Ministry of Charles R. Swindoll

Charles R. Swindoll has devoted his life to the accurate, practical teaching and application of God's Word and His grace. A pastor at heart, Chuck has served as senior pastor to congregations in Massachusetts, California, and Texas. Since 1998, he has served as the founder and senior pastor-teacher of Stonebriar Community Church in Frisco, Texas, but Chuck's listening audience extends far beyond a local church body. As a leading program in Christian broadcasting since 1979, *Insight for Living* airs in major Christian radio markets around the world, reaching people groups in languages they can understand. Chuck's extensive writing ministry has also served the body of Christ worldwide, and his leadership as president and now chancellor of Dallas Theological Seminary has helped prepare and equip a new generation of men and women for ministry. Chuck and Cynthia, his partner in life and ministry, have four grown children, ten grandchildren, and six great-grandchildren.

Published By:
IFL Publishing House
A Division of Insight for Living Ministries
Post Office Box 5000
Frisco, Texas 75034-0055

Editor in Chief: Cynthia Swindoll, President, Insight for Living Ministries
Executive Vice President: Wayne Stiles, Th.M., D.Min., Dallas Theological Seminary
Managing Editor: Barb Peil, M.A., Christian Education, Dallas Theological Seminary
Writers: John Adair, Th.M., Ph.D., Dallas Theological Seminary
Barb Peil, M.A., Christian Education, Dallas Theological Seminary
Wayne Stiles, Th.M., D.Min., Dallas Theological Seminary
Theological Editors: John Adair, Th.M., Ph.D., Dallas Theological Seminary
Derrick G. Jeter, Th.M., Dallas Theological Seminary
Content Editor: Amy L. Snedaker, B.A., English, Rhodes College
Copy Editors: Jim Craft, M.A., English, Mississippi College
Kathryn Robertson, M.A., English, Hardin-Simmons University
Project Coordinator/Editor: Melanie Munnell, M.A., Humanities, The University of Texas at Dallas
Project Coordinator, Communications: Sarah Magnoni, A.A.S., University of Wisconsin
Proofreader: Paula McCoy, B.A., English, Texas A&M University-Commerce
Designer: Laura Dubroc, B.F.A., Advertising Design, University of Louisiana at Lafayette
Production Artist: Nancy Gustine, B.F.A., Advertising Art, University of North Texas
Photos:
Todd Bolen/BiblePlaces.com: pages 13, 18, 29, 30–31, 33, 37, 41, 56, 57
Wayne Stiles: pages 10–11, 44
Isam Siam: page 73
Map page 2: Bible Mapper program and all data copyright © 2005–2010 by David P. Barrett. All rights reserved.

ISBN: 978-1-57972-903-5 (Paperback edition)
ISBN: 978-1-62655-121-3 (e-book edition)
Printed in the United States of America